Contents

LittleBrother
B O O K S

Published 2024.

Little Brother Books Ltd, Ground Floor, 23 Southernhay East, Exeter, Devon, EX1 1QL

Printed in the United Kingdom.
Little Brother Books, 77 Camden Street Lower, Dublin D02 XE80

books@littlebrotherbooks.co.uk | www.littlebrotherbooks.co.uk

The Little Brother Books trademarks, logos, email and website addresses and the Games Warrior logo and imprint are sole and exclusive properties of Little Brother Books Limited.

WELCOME TO MINECRAFT

If you're looking for adventure, excitement and the chance to get really creative, then you've come to the right place! Mojang's Minecraft is officially the biggest video game of all time, with over 300 million copies sold to date and countless dedicated players around the world.

Released in 2009, Minecraft has continued to grow and change over the years, with the most recent additions being the 1.19 The Wild and 1.20 Trails & Tales updates released in 2023. Now there are even more maps to explore, items to craft and mobs to encounter than ever before, whether you're exploring on your own or with other players.

Inside The Ultimate Guide to Minecraft you'll find everything you need to know about the game, along with tips, tricks and secrets guaranteed to impress you and your friends. There's information on how to get started if you're just beginning your journey and more advanced facts and stats for true Minecraft pros.

Minecraft is also the most watched video game on YouTube, with creators from all over the globe making their own content and sharing it with other like-minded fans.

So get ready to step into the Overworld, start building anything you can imagine and discover just how much there is to see and do in Minecraft!

Minecraft can be played on Xbox, PlayStation and Nintendo Switch consoles, as well as PC and mobile platforms.

WHAT'S NEW IN MINECRAFT

Prepare to enter a blocky universe of world-creating with Mojang's Minecraft. New content, events and updates are being released every year, so it's no wonder this video game is one of the most popular on the planet!

MINECRAFT LIVE

Minecraft Live 2023 took place on October 15, with the annual event revealing a sneak peek at the future of the game. During the livestream, players discovered what will be added to Minecraft over the coming months, including new mobs, locations and items.

NEW CONTENT

Update 1.21 adds the crafter (automated crafting) and underground Trial Chambers to the game, as well as a new mob called the breeze. This jumping enemy can shoot projectiles of wind that explode on contact, causing plenty of damage.

NEW BLOCKS

Also appearing in update 1.21 is the trial spawner, allowing players to unleash a certain number of mobs within a set time limit, as well as the new copper bulb, which emits light depending on how much oxygen is around and starts to fade as it's used up.

MINECRAFT X STAR WARS

At Minecraft Live 2023, Mojang revealed a major new piece of licensed DLC, Star Wars: Path of the Jedi. This awesome content launched on November 7 and allows players to train from Padawan to a Jedi Knight and explore characters and locations in a galaxy far, far away.

MOB VOTE

During the Minecraft 2023 Mob Vote, fans were asked to choose which creature would make it into a future version of the game: armadillo, crab or penguin. The results revealed that the armadillo was the ultimate winner with a whopping 42.3% of the vote!

CRAB — 32.5%
ARMADILLO — 42.3%
PENGUIN — 25.2%

MINECRAFT REALMS

Minecraft Realms and Realms Plus are subscription-based services letting you play online with others on your own personal server. Realms Plus subscribers recently got an upgrade, with the Dressing Room offering access to a 150+ piece catalogue of amazing content.

MILLIONS OF GAMES!

It's been revealed that Minecraft has now sold more than 300 million copies so far, making it the biggest-selling video game of all time. That's not too bad at all, considering that Mojang launched Minecraft over 15 years ago!

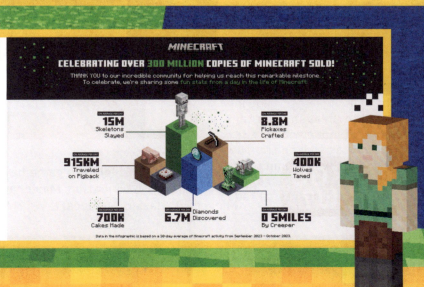

MINECRAFT
CELEBRATING OVER 300 MILLION COPIES OF MINECRAFT SOLD!
THANK YOU to our incredible community for helping us reach this remarkable milestone. To celebrate, we're sharing some fun stats from a day in the life of Minecraft.

- **15M** Skeletons Slayed
- **8.8M** Pickaxes Crafted
- **915KM** Traveled on Pigback
- **400K** Wolves Tamed
- **700K** Cakes Made
- **6.7M** Diamonds Discovered
- **0 SMILES** By Creeper

Data in the infographic is based on a 30-day average of Minecraft activity from September 2023 – October 2023.

HOW TO PLAY MINECRAFT

You can play Minecraft on all sorts of different gaming platforms, from mobile to consoles. If you're new to Mojang's blocky world, then here's everything you need to know to get started on your own epic journey!

1 Before you begin a new Minecraft game, you'll need to create a Microsoft account. You may need the help of an adult to do so, or if you already have an account, you can just use your existing login details.

2 From the main menu screen, you can select what sort of game mode you'd like to choose from (see pages 8–9), check out Minecraft Realms or select other options. Helpful, funny and odd messages also pop up on this screen!

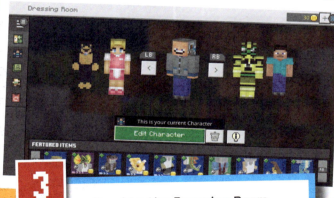

3 Head to the Dressing Room and you'll be able to change the appearance of your in-game character. It's possible to swap and play around with almost any element of your digital avatar, from clothes and armour to weapons and tools.

DID YOU KNOW? Other versions of Mojang's game have been released over the years including Minecraft Education, Minecraft China, Minecraft: Pocket Edition, Minecraft Classic, Minecraft: Wii U Edition, Minecraft 4K and more!

4 The Minecraft Marketplace (pages 32–33) is the place for players to buy and sell items using Minecoins. Check out all of the various Skin Packs, Texture Packs, Worlds and Mash-Up Packs on offer.

5 Once you've settled on the final look for your avatar and selected a game mode, it's time to explore the Overworld. Maps include pre-set and randomly generated levels that are just waiting to be explored.

6 By looking around maps, collecting items and encountering various mobs, you'll start to get a feel for the game. You may not last very long on your very first night in Minecraft, but you'll soon learn how to survive!

7 When you die in the game, you'll respawn at a random point in the Overworld. It's possible to lose your life if you're attacked and run out of health points, if you fall too far, or if you encounter a hazard such as lava.

PRACTISE MAKES PERFECT!

The best way to become a better Minecraft player is to practise again and again. You won't get it right every time, but all of the tools, items and resources you need to become a pro are included in the game. Now go for it!

GAME MODES

There are three main game modes in Minecraft: Survival, Creative and Adventure. Each one offers players a different experience, either on their own or with others. Check them all out to find out which one you prefer!

GET STARTED

From the main menu, select Play to create a brand new world or revist an existing one. Each option allows you to pick Survival or Creative modes, then customise your game settings however you want.

SURVIVAL MODE

Survival is the standard game mode where you start from scratch with no supplies at all. Players also only have limited health and need to find and build shelter, hunt for food and other items and avoid aggressive mobs.

CREATIVE MODE

In Creative mode, you're in total control of the game and can do almost anything you want! You'll have unlimited health and any resources you like, it's also possible to destroy any block with one hit and fly by double-jumping.

ADVENTURE MODE

Adventure mode is handy if you only want to explore maps and play mini-games. Blocks can't be placed, but weapons and other items can still be used against mobs and other players.

DID YOU KNOW?

Some blocks and items in Creative mode can only be obtained on certain platforms. These include the spectral arrow in the Java Edition of the game and firework rockets in the Bedrock Edition.

MAKE A HOUSE!

In both Survival and Creative modes, players can start building and crafting (see pages 14–17). That usually begins with a small house or other shelter, constructed from any nearby resources that can be found.

COMMANDS

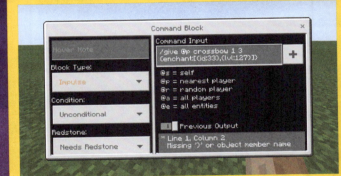

Commands are a handy tool that can completely transform your Minecraft experience. Selecting 'Allow Cheats' opens up all sorts of options, massively changing the rules of the game for all players.

MINECRAFT SERVERS

It's possible to play Survival and Creative modes in multiplayer, but you'll need to have a working internet connection to do so. Once you're logged into the Minecraft servers, you can join forces to build and battle!

HARDCORE MODE

The Java Edition of Minecraft also adds Spectator and Hardcore options. In Spectator mode, players can fly around the Overworld, but can't interact with it. Hardcore is a variant of Survival that's very difficult and players are unable to respawn!

DID YOU KNOW?

Commands can be entered in the in-game Chat window and require players to enter specific words to activate them. Successful commands can include giving players new abilities, switching the camera angle, removing spawn points from a world, applying damage to certain mobs and much more.

NEW BIOMES

The two most recent updates to Minecraft have added three distinct new biomes to the game. Each of these worlds includes previously unseen blocks, items, structures, mobs and so much more to discover!

THE DEEP DARK

The 1.19 The Wild update added the Deep Dark, a cave biome that generates far below the mountains of the Overworld. Here you'll discover jagged peaks, snowy slopes and huge caverns that are only lit by glow lichen or lava.

GOING UNDERGROUND

The Deep Dark tends to be covered in large patches of sculk blocks and sculk veins. It's the only biome where ancient cities can generate, but other structures, such as monster rooms and strongholds, can also be found.

THE WARDEN!

No mobs spawn in this biome, but if a player triggers a sculk shrieker block, the fearsome warden may appear. You can find out all about this powerful new mob on page 25, but for now, just avoid the creature if you encounter it!

DID YOU KNOW?

Developer Mojang was originally planning to add another new mob to the 1.19 The Wild update – fireflies! However, some species of the creature are poisonous to certain frogs in real-life, so they were left out.

MANGROVE SWAMP

The second new biome to be added in the 1.19 The Wild update was Mangrove Swamp. As its name suggests, this is a variant of the standard Swamp biome and generates next to warmer areas such as Jungles and Deserts.

SWAMP THINGS

Here players will discover mud and grass blocks, with leaves and vines that have a light green colour. The only friendly animals you'll find here are warm frogs and tropical fish, but there are plenty of mobs to battle.

MAKE A BOAT

In the Mangrove Swamp you'll find mangrove trees to make mangrove boats, as well as all kinds of new blocks, items and structures. Note that swamp huts and mushrooms do not generate naturally in this biome.

CHERRY GROVE

Introduced in the 1.20 Trails and Tales update, Cherry Grove is similar to Meadows biome. Both have the same sort of vegetation and layouts, plus emerald ores that can be found in high places in the locations.

WHAT LIES BENEATH....

Cherry Grove is the only place where cherry trees generate and the biome is home to infested block blobs. When exploring beneath mountains, you'll usually discover that the caves of the Deep Dark can be found below.

NEW BLOCKS

Thanks to the 1.19 The Wild update and 1.20 Trails and Tales update, in 2023, there are all sorts of new blocks for players to try out in Minecraft. In total 39 additional blocks are now available, but here's our pick of the most unique.

FROGLIGHT

When a frog eats a tiny magma cube, a froglight can be obtained. Three different versions of this light-emitting block can be found.

MUD

Located throughout Mangrove Swamp biomes, mud blocks can be used for crafting purposes or converted into clay by using pointed dropstone.

DID YOU KNOW?

Mud already existed as an item, although only as a fluid, in Minecraft Earth. The 1.19 The Wild update then added it to the game as a solid block with many more handy uses.

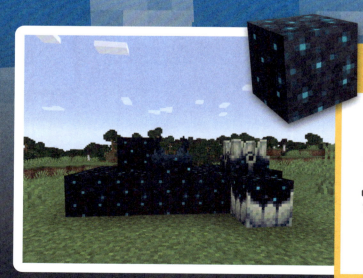

SCULK

This block with glowing spots covers the Deep Dark and drops experience when broken by a tool not enchanted with Silk Touch.

BAMBOO

Head to the Mangrove Swamp to find this block. It can be broken by hand and used to create bamboo planks and for fuel.

PIGLIN HEAD

This block is one of seven entity heads that can be used for decoration or for wearing. Piglin heads are always dropped by a piglin when it dies.

PINK PETALS

Only located in Cherry Grove biomes, pink petals can be gathered by hand or harvested with shears. They're handy for decorating and crafting into a pink dye.

SNIFFER EGG

Use a brush on suspicious sand or breed two sniffers together to get this item. A sniffer egg will slowly hatch into a baby sniffer when placed in a world.

TORCHFLOWER

When sniffers finish digging, they sometimes drop torchflower seeds. These can then be planted and farmed and used to breed sniffers and chickens.

CRAFTING GUIDE

1 If you haven't tried crafting yet, it couldn't be easier. Start by opening your inventory to see a list of items you've collected on your travels. You can also find chests in each map that contain useful goodies.

2 To begin, mine some wood by breaking nearby trees. Pick up the blocks that are dropped and add four of them into the 2x2 crafting grid in your inventory. This is called a recipe and it gives you wood planks.

3 Select the wood planks and add them to your inventory below. Now place four wood plank blocks in the crafting grid and the new recipe will create a crafting table, one of the most useful items in Minecraft!

4 Place the crafting table on the ground in the Overworld and then open it up. Your inventory screen will now have changed, showing a 3x3 grid on the left-hand side which can be used to make more complicated recipes.

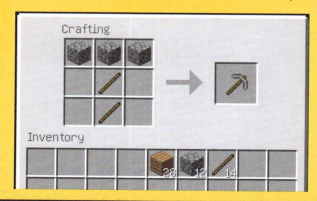

5 Try making a much more useful item by dropping two wood planks into the crafting grid to make four sticks. Then place one stick in the grid with two wood planks above as shown. Now you've constructed your first wooden sword!

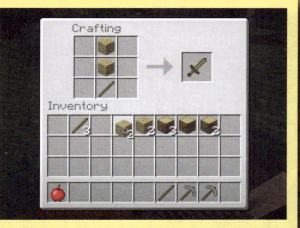

6 Once you've made some basic tools such as a sword, pickaxe and shovel, you'll have a much easier time staying alive and mining even more items in the Overworld. Try using different materials for constructing stronger tools.

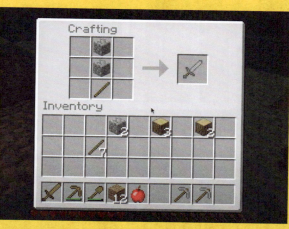

7 Every time you create a new item for the first time, it's added to your recipe book. Recipes can be found in your inventory, which eventually adds various tabs such as Blocks, Tools, Brewing, Dyes, Defence and more!

DID YOU KNOW?

The ability to craft was first added into Minecraft back in the 0.31 update for the game in 2009-2010. The only recipe available at the time was the option to turn an apple into an arrow. There are currently 379 craftable items in the game, with more being added with each new update!

For a guide to some of the most essential recipes you'll need in Minecraft, just head to **pages 16-17**. The items listed range from the basics right up to creations for real Minecraft pros!

TOP 10

ESSENTIAL RECIPES

There are all kinds of useful of items that can be created in Minecraft by using recipes. Here are 10 of the most essential that you'll need to be able to make if you want to master the Overworld!

SPYGLASS

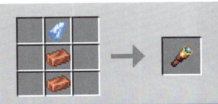

This handy item is made from two copper ingots and an amethyst shard. To get those you'll need to do plenty of exploring and mining underground.

CAMPFIRE

If you're new to Minecraft you'll need to know how to cook food to survive. A simple campfire is crafted from three logs, three sticks and a piece of coal.

RED NETHER BRICK

If you've already explored the Nether, then you can make this special decorative block. Add two netherrack to two nether wart and you're good to go.

HONEYCOMB BLOCK

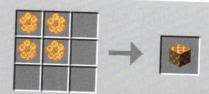

If you have four bottles of honey, then it's time to make a honeycomb block. This item slows down anything passing through it and they can also be stuck to other blocks.

POWERED RAILS

There's no electricity in Minecraft, but there are ways of making things move. To craft powered rails, combine six gold ingots, a stick and redstone dust.

MAP

The Overworld is so huge, you'll definitely need to know where you're going! Craft a map with eight pieces of paper and a compass that uses iron redstone.

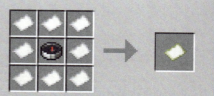

BLUE ICE

Collect nine pieces of ice and combine them to create packed ice. Now add nine of those blocks together to create super-slippery blue ice!

LIGHTNING ROD

A recent addition to the game, the lightning rod can prevent your buildings from burning down if struck. Use three copper ingots to make this useful item.

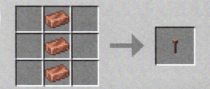

MAGMA CREAM

Grab blaze powder from blaze rods and mix them with slime balls. This will make magma cream, a handy item for various potions and crafting recipes.

RESPAWN ANCHOR

Super-charge your exploration of the Nether with the respawn anchor. Trade with a piglin to get obsidian and mine glowstone to create handy respawn points!

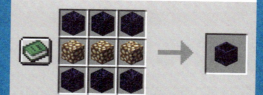

QUICK BUILD:
AUTOMATED
CHICKEN FARM

Follow the 10 quick and easy steps in each of these guides and you too will be able to construct some amazing builds. First up is a handy machine that can create an endless supply of food for you!

1
To start off, select a map seed and enter a world. Find a flat piece of ground and place a double chest next to a hopper.

2
Next, attach eight glass blocks around the hopper, but ensure you keep the central section leading down to it clear of any items.

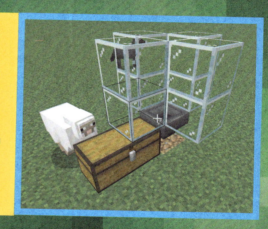

3
Now stand on top of the glass blocks and look down. Add a stone slab inside, so that it sits on top of the hopper.

4
Select a dispenser block and attach it next to the hopper, then tip a bucket of lava into the empty block space.

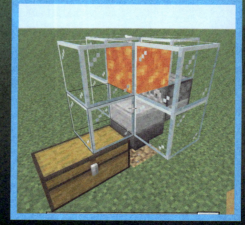

DID YOU KNOW?

This build uses chicken spawn eggs to create tasty food, but try placing different types of eggs inside the farm and see what happens!

18

5

Head round the back of your build and add two more hoppers. These should be stacked on top of each other.

6

Add eight more glass blocks to your construction, placing them around the top hopper. Throw lots and lots of chicken spawn eggs inside.

7

Place a wood block with a comparator on top of it next to the hoppers, then add two more hoppers on the other side.

8

Go into your inventory and add as many non-stackable items as you like. These can include things like weapons and fishing rods.

9

Now place the non-stackable items into the hoppers on the side of the build. Make sure your comparator switches are set up as shown.

10

The Automated Chicken Farm will now start to work and convert all of the poultry into ready-cooked food for you to eat. Yum, yum!

NEW FRIENDLY MOBS

Not all mobs are hostile and some are in fact very friendly indeed! Take a look at five cute critters that were added in the 1.19 The Wild update and 1.20 Trails & Tales update and find out how they can help you on your travels.

The 1.19 The Wild update and 1.20 Trails & Tales update were major updates for Minecraft and both were released in 2023. These upgrades added five new passive mobs to the game, as well as the lumbering warden (see page 25)!

ALLAY

Found near pillager outposts, allays are flying mobs that deliver items to players who give them something. They can also be summoned if they hear a note block playing. Teleport through a Nether portal and your allay will even come with you!

DID YOU KNOW?

Allays were due to be added to the 1.16 The Nether update in 2020, but eventually made it into the game after the mob vote in Minecraft Live 2021.

FROG

Groups of two to five frogs often spawn in Swamp and Mangrove Swamp biomes. They eat slimes and if you give them a magma cube they will produce a froglight. There are three different frog variants to find in the game.

TADPOLE

Hatched from frogspawn, tadpoles are an aquatic baby mob that can be collected in a bucket of water. They'll follow a player holding a slimeball, but quickly die on land. Unlike frogs, tadpoles are hunted by axolotls!

CAMEL

Spawned into desert biomes, camels can be tamed and saddled, allowing up to two players to ride them at a time. As camels are so tall, their riders won't be attacked by some shorter hostile mobs.

Camels also have a unique ability that can sometimes come in handy when travelling around the Overworld. The mob is able to step up 1.5 block-high walls and fences without automatically stopping to do so.

SNIFFER

Sniffers don't spawn naturally and can only be hatched from sniffer eggs. They sniff around for food and dig out seeds from dirt, grass and moss blocks. The mob can also be bred using torchflower seeds, creating a snifflet!

15 MOST DANGEROUS MOBS

There are all kinds of different mobs to be encountered in Minecraft and not all of them are friendly! Check out the full line-up of the most dangerous enemies lurking in the Overworld, the Nether and the End so you're fully prepared when you meet them...

15
ZOMBIFIED PIGLIN

This undead version of the piglin can be found in the Nether. They tend to ignore players, but will attack with their golden swords if provoked.

14
ENDERMAN

Located in the Overworld, the Nether and the End, this creepy mob can do some serious damage. One look into their weird eyes is enough to set them off!

13
CHARGED CREEPER

When lightning strikes within four blocks of a creeper, a charged creeper is created. This super-explosive mob is best avoided, if at all possible.

12 BLAZE

This hostile mob spawns in Nether fortresses and is the only source of blaze rods. They attack anyone who approaches them with a volley of fireballs.

11 GHAST

A floating ghost-like mob that lives in the Nether. They make weird crying sounds and launch powerful explosive fireballs at nearby players.

10 ELDER GUARDIAN

The strongest aquatic mob in Minecraft, elder guardians have 40 health hearts and three attack modes. Only the toughest will survive an encounter with them!

9 WITHER SKELETON

Another resident of Nether fortresses, wither skeletons are armed with a sword and a lethal status effect. Get hit by one and you'll be affected by their undead ability for 10 seconds.

DID YOU KNOW?

Wither skeletons are the only source of wither skeleton skulls, that can be used for decorating builds. They're also the only source of renewable coal available in the game and have a 2.5% chance of spawning wearing a carved pumpkin during Halloween!

8 VINDICATOR

If one of this hostile mob spots you, it will call for other vindicators to join in and help it. Even more deadly than that is a vindicator riding a ravager!

7 PIGLIN BRUTE

Another piglin variant, this challenging mob pops up in Nether bastion locations. Groups of them can cause massive amounts of damage, so take them out from a distance.

6 EVOKER

Only spawning in illager raids or woodland mansions, evokers use spell-like magic attacks. They'll unleash evoker fangs and vexes to quickly drain your energy.

4 IRON GOLEM

Although a mostly neutral mob, iron golems can be formidable foes if you're not careful. They often patrol villages, so keep your distance when near them.

5 RAVAGER

This mob can cause serious destruction by running, biting and smashing into enemies. They spawn alongside illagers in raids and can be briefly stunned by blocking them with a shield.

3 ENDER DRAGON

The final boss in Minecraft, this beast is found in the End and has a 200 health bar. You'll need to take out the crystals it uses to recharge before launching your own attack.

DID YOU KNOW?

Some dangerous mobs in Minecraft often ride around on non-hostile mobs. These animal mounts can include chickens, skeleton horses, spiders and more. Mojang was going to add in a zombie horse at one point, which would have been super-scary!

2 THE WARDEN

Added in the recent 1.19 update, wardens are incredibly powerful to beat. They have a sonic boom attack and are immune to fire, lava and knockback effects.

1 THE WITHER

The most dangerous mob in Minecraft, the wither is a formidable enemy. It has special armour, near invulnerability and shoots explosive skulls. You have been warned!

TAMING AND BREEDING GUIDE

Did you know, with so many animal mobs in the Overworld, it's actually possible to tame and breed many different kinds?

This guide shows you how to do just that and details the items you can get as rewards.

SADDLE UP!

Horses, donkeys and mules don't require items to tame them. Interact with the animals a few times and put a saddle on their backs to ride them. Use a lead to take them home and ensure they don't wander away.

FURRY FRIENDS

Give a wolf a bone and it will follow you around until a red collar appears around its neck. Use raw salmon or raw cod to tempt cats, but approach them slowly or they may become spooked and run off.

PARROT PERCH

It's possible to tame parrots by feeding them seeds. Once you've done so, you can tell the bird to perch on your shoulders or fly around with you as you explore a map. Just don't give parrots cookies as they're poisonous!

Some animals need to be tamed before breeding. Here's a list of which ones and what food item you'll need to make that happen.

Wolves (Tamed)	Any raw or cooked meat other than fish
Cats (Tamed) and ocelots	Raw cod or raw salmon
Horses and donkeys (Tamed)	Golden apples and golden carrots
Llamas (Tamed)	Hay bales
Sheep, cows, goats and mooshrooms	Wheat
Pigs	Carrots, potatoes or beetroot
Chickens	Seeds (will also produce eggs on their own without any influence)
Rabbits	Dandelions, carrots or golden carrots
Turtles	Seagrass
Pandas	Bamboo – you must have eight bamboo blocks within a radius of five blocks of both pandas
Foxes	Sweet berries or glow berries
Bees	Flowers
Frogs	Slimeball
Axolotls	Bucket of tropical fish
Camels	Cactus
Striders	Warped fungus
Hoglins	Crimson fungus
Sniffers	Torchflower seeds

BREEDING PAIRS

To breed animals, start by ensuring two of the mob are close to each other and they'll then enter 'love mode.' Small red hearts will appear above the creatures and a baby or an egg will then appear.

BABY MOBS

Baby animals can also be created by using a spawn egg on an adult, which even works on zombie mobs. It takes about 20 minutes for a baby to fully grow, but you can speed it up by giving them their breeding food.

DID YOU KNOW?

Baby polar bears grow into adults, but can't be bred. Neither can squids, glow squids or dolphins in the Bedrock version of the game.

QUICK BUILD:
CREATE AN EPIC
DESERT BASE

Desert biomes contain plenty of empty temples, but they're usually pretty drab inside and out. Use the 10 simple steps on these pages and you'll be able to convert one of those dusty buildings into an awesome base!

1

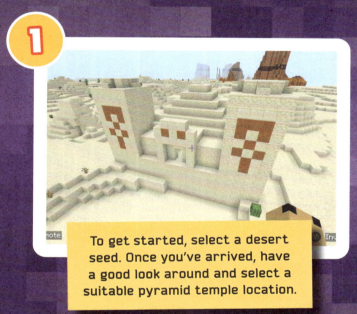

To get started, select a desert seed. Once you've arrived, have a good look around and select a suitable pyramid temple location.

2

Before you begin, find the hidden treasure room. You'll need to deactivate the pressure plate or the TNT trap will explode!

3

Next, head to the largest room you can find and clear out some space. You'll want to give yourself enough room to work in.

4

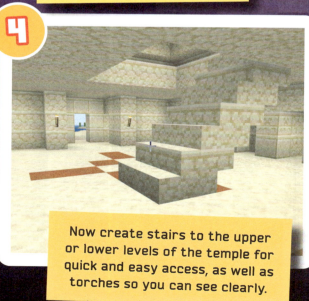

Now create stairs to the upper or lower levels of the temple for quick and easy access, as well as torches so you can see clearly.

5 On the upper floor, try making your own bedroom packed with any items you like. These can include armour, pictures, enchanted books and more!

6

Head outside and work on the exterior of the temple next. Wooden stair blocks can be used to build rooftops and you can try adding stairs and lanterns too.

7

A kitchen area adds a really great touch to any desert base! Use furnaces for an oven, a cauldron with water for a sink, a sign and patterned floor tiles.

8 The deactivated treasure room can now be improved by placing a ladder on the wall for easy access, torches for light and precious blocks such as gold and diamond.

9

A hollowed-out tower can be a handy look out post. Place stairs on the inside walls to reach it, plus a simple balcony and a spyglass for great views.

10 Complete your epic desert base with a fun chill-out area. A massive TV, a sprawling sofa, bookcases, a table and a rug make great finishing touches!

DID YOU KNOW?

Desert temples always contain four hidden loot chests to be located. There's also a secret buried room to be found, if you look hard enough. Thanks to the 1.20 Trails & Tales update, you can perform archaeology in this room, using the new brush tool to find precious fossils and more!

NEW TOOLS & ITEMS

Both the 1.19 The Wild update and 1.20 Trails & Tales update added all sorts of new stuff to Minecraft, giving players even more options than ever before. Check out some of the most recent tools and items that are now at your disposal.

Launched on June 7, 2022, 1.19 The Wild update was a major release for Mojang's game, bringing with it a host of exciting extras. These included the bucket of tadpoles, echo shards, goat horn, disc fragment and much more.

ECHO SHARDS

Echo shards can be found in ancient cities and a crafting recipe using eight pieces with a compass in the centre can create a recovery compass. This handy item will then point to the location of your last death and any loot you left behind.

MANGROVE BOAT

Thanks to new Mangrove Swamp biomes, players can now craft a mangrove boat. This is basically the same as a standard boat, but constructed from five mangrove planks that are dark brown in appearance.

GOAT HORNS

When they die, goats now drop goat horns and there are eight different versions to find. They are the Ponder, Sing, Seek, Feel, Admire, Call, Yearn and Dream horns, each of which makes its own unique sound.

The 1.20 Trails & Tales update dropped on June 7, 2023, giving players even more tools and items to aid them in their adventures. New arrivals such as a brush, pitcher pod, pottery shards, smithing templates and torchflower seeds are now available.

DID YOU KNOW?

Mojang was going to add stone chests in 1.19 The Wild, but ultimately decided to leave them out of that update.

NEW BRUSH TOOL

Archaeology finally arrived in the 1.20 Trails & Tales update, allowing players to locate historical items inside some blocks with a brush. The tool can be crafted from a feather, a copper ingot and a stick and can also receive enchantments.

PITCHER POD

The pitcher pod is a large and ancient seed sometimes dropped by sniffers when digging. Place one on farmland and it'll grow through three stages and can be used to breed chickens and tame parrots.

ARMOUR TRIMS

There are 16 armour trims located in various structures that can be used to decorate armour using certain minerals. They can even be duplicated by using seven diamonds and a block based on what the template is.

MINECRAFT
MARKETPLACE

If you're looking to enhance your gaming experience, then be sure to check out Minecraft Marketplace. Here you can grab all kinds of awesome skin packs, maps, mini games and community-created content!

The Minecraft Marketplace is exclusive to the Bedrock Edition of the game and can be accessed from the main menu. Once in the store, players can add Minecoins (or Tokens on PlayStation 4) to their virtual wallets and start spending.

As it costs real money to buy Minecoins, ask a grown-up for permission first!

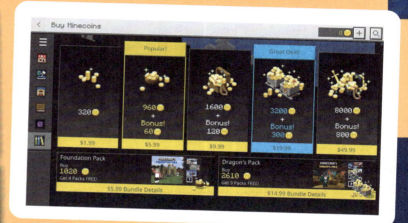

PURCHASE PACKS

There are all kinds of items to be purchased in Minecraft Marketplace, many of which have been created by fans themselves. The in-game store allows players to buy Skin Packs, Texture Packs, Worlds and Mash-up Packs.

MINECOINS

Minecoins can be purchased with real-world currency or bought through Minecraft Marketplace. The coins can then be exchanged for items costing that amount, with some exclusives only available for a limited time.

EXTRA DLC

Skin Packs are custom skins that can be used in single player and multiplayer games and some are free. The World category offers up pre-built maps to play on such as Adventure Maps, Mini-Games and Survival Spawns.

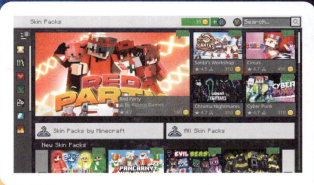

Texture Packs let players customise the look of worlds, sounds and items and the shape of some mobs. If you're after all-in-one bundles, then Mash-up Packs combine worlds, textures and skins into a single purchase.

FAMILIAR FACES

There's a Pop Culture tab in Minecraft Marketplace, where you can find licensed DLC featuring some of your favourite characters. This has included the likes of Star Wars, Disney, TMNT, Sonic the Hedgehog and more!

MY CONTENT

The My Content section of Minecraft Marketplace shows all the items you've purchased and details of any current Realms Plus subscriptions. This is the place to head to if you want to see what you own so far.

DID YOU KNOW?

Before Minecraft Marketplace was introduced, all Texture Packs and Skin Packs that were available for purchase had to be bought with real money!

Like creating your own Minecraft content? Then share it on Minecraft Marketplace and make money! Design your own skins for others to buy or become a Marketplace Creator if you have maps and other items to sell.

TIPS AND TRICKS YOU NEED TO KNOW!

Are you ready to take your Minecraft gaming to the next level? Once you've learned the basics, prepare to go deeper with these handy tips and tricks that are guaranteed to make you a pro in no time at all!

LOTS OF LAVA

Keep track of where lava is in a world, as a bucket full of red-hot magma is perfect furnace fuel. Lava can also be used to create obsidian, a super-rare block that can't be crafted using a recipe!

CREATE CUSTOM DOG COLLARS

Having a pack of tamed dogs comes in handy when hunting. It's possible to give your dogs their own personalities by using dyes to change the colour of each canine's collar!

STAY SAFE IN A MUSHROOM BIOME

If you want to stay safe most of the time, just head to a Mushroom biome. Mobs won't spawn here at night and don't appear in the cave systems, so you won't be attacked.

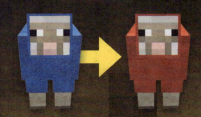

MAKE RED SHEEP

This is tricky, but can be done with practise. If you can get an Evoker near a blue sheep, it will wiggle its arms, say 'wololo' and then turn the sheep red. This is a reference to another video game, Age of Empires.

STOP MOB SPAWNERS WORKING

Mob spawners continually create enemies, until you destroy the block. However, if you place flaming torches on each side and one on top, that will prevent more mobs from appearing.

KEEP CREEPERS AWAY WITH CATS

You can make friends with lots of animals in Minecraft, but cats may be the most useful. If you have enough felines, they can actually scare off nearby Creepers, as the green mobs seem to be really afraid of them!

Position: 227, 74, -179

ZOMBIES LOVE TURTLE EGGS

Zombies just can't get enough of turtle eggs! This comes in handy if you're making a zombified piglin farm. Put the egg in the middle of a spawn platform and place a hole just before it. The mob will then fall into it and drop gold.

LLAMAS CAN CARRY A LOT OF STUFF

Breed llamas to increase their strength and use their other handy ability. Click on a llama while holding a chest and the chest becomes their inventory space, with 15 available slots to store stuff.

TOP 10

RAREST MINECRAFT SKINS

You can buy all sorts of amazing character skins in Minecraft, but some are very hard to find and usually only available for a limited time. Here are 10 of the rarest skins ever released for Mojang's game that are now all gone for good!

SPIDER-MAN

Available from 2014 to 2015, the Marvel Spider-Man pack included seven amazing skins. Of those, it's the classic version of the web-slinger that's a standout in the limited edition set.

THE SIMPSONS

All five of the animated characters were included in The Simpsons skin pack that was only available for the Xbox edition of Minecraft. If you managed to grab this yellow-skinned family back from 2015 to 2017, consider yourself very lucky.

ENDER DRAGON

Mojang releases plenty of its own character packs too. The first of five birthday skin packs arrived in 2013 for the Xbox 360 Edition of Minecraft and it featured an awesome Ender Dragon skin!

DALEK

This licensed skin pack is unusual, as it has a selection of Daleks that aren't shaped like the standard player model. The Doctor Who villain was available in different colours and was released on Xbox One in 2014.

EVIL LEMMY

This exclusive Halloween pack came with a whole host of creepy skins. One of the weirdest has to be Evil Lemmy, who has a black blocky body and a giant scary eye for a head!

MINECON 2011 CAPES

Special character capes are sometimes as rare as some skins. The first exclusive capes came out in 2011 to celebrate Minecon and were re-released later on in two limited edition skin packs.

TONY HAWK

This skateboarding legend made it into a special pack of skins released in 2012 to advertise the XBLA arcade game event. Although he didn't come with his own deck or any cool moves, the skins were definitely a must-have for Tony Hawk fans.

SUPER MARIO

The stars of Nintendo's games often pop up as skins, but this Super Mario-themed pack was one of the best. Released in 2016 on Wii U and Nintendo Switch, it included Mario, Luigi, Princess Daisy and more.

ICE PIONEER

In 2016, Mojang released a Minecon skin pack, themed around features developers were adding to the game. The pack included the Ice Pioneer skin from the iceberg biome, one that's very detailed and hard to find.

ENDERMAN CAPE

The rarest item in this list is the Enderman Cape. Available for a limited time in 2016, the cape featured classic Enderman colours with purple eyes and only a handful of Minecraft players have it!

DID YOU KNOW?

Seven unique villagers skins were added to the game by Mojang in 2014 to celebrate April Fools' Day!

QUICK BUILD: SUPER SORTING MACHINE

It's possible to build all kinds of useful gadgets in Minecraft with just a few basic blocks. Try your hand at making a Super Sorting Machine and you'll soon discover just how handy this clever device can be!

1

First, find somewhere flat with plenty of space to work. Dig a hole one block down and place a chest on top of two hoppers.

2

Move around the build and select a dispenser block. This should sit next to the hopper without the chest on it.

3

Now construct a 3x3 tower using glass blocks. Be sure to cover the dispenser and one hopper, but not the chest.

4

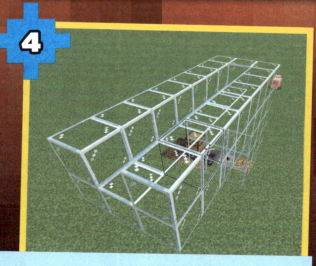

Use more glass blocks to make a flat channel area on top of the tower. Add a glass block at one end, keeping the other end open.

5

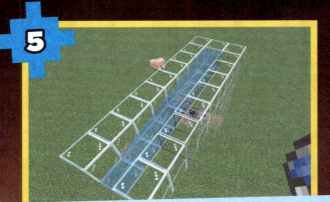

Grab your bucket and pour water into the open channel and fill it up. You don't need to worry about it flowing out of the end though!

6

Underneath the flat top area, quickly replace the glass blocks in the channel with hoppers. In total you'll need six hoppers in a row.

7

Now add three more rows of six hoppers below. This should then give you four rows, with six hoppers in each.

8

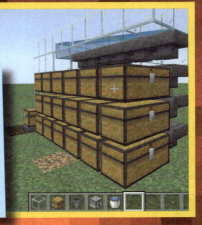

On one side of the build place six large chests in a row next to the hoppers. In total you should have 18 double chests.

9

Place a single chest and a comparator next to the two hoppers, as shown, and fill them with non-stackable items such as weapons and armour.

10

When you place any items into the single chest, they'll automatically be sorted into the double chests and stored for when you need them most!

DID YOU KNOW? Placing two single chests next to each other automatically creates a large chest. A small chest has 27 inventory slots, while a large chest has room for 54 items. From December 24–26, all chests have their textures changed and become Christmas chests!

THE BEST MINECRAFT
ADVENTURE MAPS

Minecraft Marketplace is the place to check out if you're looking to download cool extras to enhance your games (see page 32). There are all sorts of amazing maps and textures to grab, so here's our pick of some of the very best!

10 YEARS OF MINECRAFT

This free map was created by Blockworks to celebrate Minecraft's 10th anniversary in 2021. Add it to your collection and you can ride a mine cart through a museum packed with secrets and hidden Easter eggs.

THE REDSTONE TEMPLE

Created by Gamemode One, this free map is for anyone who's a fan of classic portal games. Make your way through different puzzle rooms within an old temple, guided by a mysterious voice, until you discover all of the secrets inside.

TAME MY DRAGON

Giggle Block Studios designed a map costing 1,170 coins that lets players take control of all kinds of dragons. Each dragon has various special abilities, such as the power to breathe fire and swim fast underwater.

RAINBOW PARK

Priced at just 660 coins, this massive Minecraft adventure map includes a theme park with fully functioning rides! Try out three different roller coasters, a Ferris wheel, a drop tower, a weird magic show and all kinds of other attractions.

ANCIENT EGYPT

This free Ancient Egypt map was created by Fall Studios. Embark on a tour through a sprawling desert, dig up pyramids, find hidden treasures, dodge four new mobs and try on six exclusive character skins.

MONSTERS OF THE DEEP

Developer Noxcrew designed this map that sends players on an epic underwater quest. Solve the mystery of why an undersea base has lost power and battle huge monster bosses with a trident, all for only 830 coins.

DID YOU KNOW?

Maps can be placed into item frames so they can be viewed together!

PARKOUR SCHOOL

In Parkour School, you can practise your skills with 15 unique challenges, learning how to leap, crouch and time your moves to perfection. The map costs 660 coins and comes with new skins too.

FARM LIFE

This free map combines Minecraft and farming in one amazing world. Created by PixleHeads, Farm Life features upgradeable tractors and harvesters, over 50 trees and crops to grow, multiple mobs to breed and so much more!

MINECRAFT
DUNGEONS

Launched in 2020, Minecraft Dungeons is a spin-off game that takes place in the Overworld of Minecraft. If you're looking for an awesome hack-and-slash dungeon crawler to play with your friends, then be sure to check this out!

Minecraft Dungeons is currently available on Nintendo Switch, PlayStation 4, PC, Xbox One and Xbox Series X and Series S.

Instead of mining or building, Minecraft Dungeons takes players on an action-packed adventure through multiple levels, with randomly generated monsters to tackle, challenging puzzles to solve and tough bosses to beat.

DID YOU KNOW?

LEGO 21163 The Redstone Battle is a set based on Minecraft Dungeons. The model includes minifigures of Valorie, Hex, Hal and Adriene, plus the Redstone Monstrosity and the Redstone Golem!

The opening cutscene tells the story of Archie, a villager who stumbles upon an artifact known as the Orb of Dominance. He's transformed into the evil Arch-Illager and players have to defeat this Overworld menace.

There's no class system in Minecraft Dungeons and players can use any weapons or armour they find in the levels. The more times you tackle the game, the more awesome upgrades and items you'll find hidden within each stage.

The game can be played in single-player mode, but it's more fun to try local or multiplayer co-op. Teaming up with friends makes for a more satisfying experience, plus you'll be able to progress much further into the game!

There have been six DLC packs released for Minecraft Dungeons so far, which continue the game's story with new content.

An Ultimate DLC Bundle can also be bought and includes a special Hero Cape, two player skins and a chicken pet!

Jungle Awakens

Howling Peaks

Hidden Depths

Echoing Void

New Season Adventures have also been added, with Cloudy Climbs being the first. Scale a mysterious tower, solve its mysteries and defeat hordes of enemies to receive more than 45 exclusive rewards.

MINECRAFT
LEGENDS

The most recent addition to Mojang's line-up of titles, Minecraft Legends launched in 2023 and is a real-time action strategy game. Team up with your mates to battle enemies or choose to fight each other in a special PvP mode!

Minecraft Legends tells the story of a war taking place between the forces of the Overworld and the piglins of the Nether. Only by destroying a number of portals can players put an end to the invasion.

DID YOU KNOW?

The Great Hog boss appears at The Well of Fates and must be defeated in order to beat the game. Do so and all remaining piglins and their structures will disappear from the Overworld.

In multiplayer mode, players work together in order to beat their foes. This can include building a protective maze around your base, gathering resources, collecting redstone and preparing for an attack.

Minecraft Legends' PvP cross-platform mode lets up to eight players, split into two teams, capture and destroy their opponent's base, while building up their own. Matches last between 20 and 30 minutes until a winner is victorious!

The game is available on Nintendo Switch, PlayStation 4, PlayStation 5, PC, Xbox One and Xbox Series X/S. Single player and multiplayer modes are included, allowing you to join forces with your friends.

Each level of the game has plenty of secrets, so you'll need to explore stages thoroughly in order to uncover all that is hidden. Watch out for rampaging piglins though, as these tough enemies can easily overwhelm you.

Purchase the Minecraft Legends Deluxe Skin Pack to boost your collection of outfits. The set includes one hero skin and five mount skins.

New challenges are added to the game each month, with rewards for players who complete them. These can include special character skins, unique items, downloadable content and mini-games.

At Minecraft Live 2023, Mojang revealed details of new content for the game. This included the ability to hop into battle on a frog mount, the addition of mysterious witches, the piglin air chopper and much more!

Frog Mount

Piglin Air Chopper

Witches

TOP 10

MINECRAFT YOUTUBERS

Many YouTubers create Minecraft videos, but some are in a different league altogether. Find out who the top 10 current Minecraft YouTube superstars are and just how many fans they actually have!

LDSHADOWLADY
7.05 MILLION SUBS

10 Also known as Elizabeth 'Lizzie' D, LDShadowLady began creating Minecraft content back in 2010. Her videos feature a mix of regular content and other games, but it's really Minecraft that's still the main focus of her channel.

EYSTREEM
7.1 MILLION SUBS

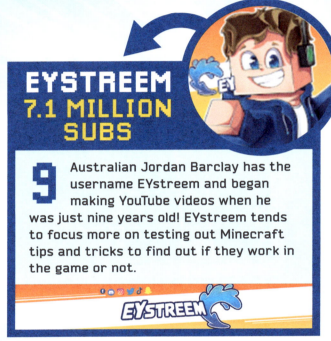

9 Australian Jordan Barclay has the username EYstreem and began making YouTube videos when he was just nine years old! EYstreem tends to focus more on testing out Minecraft tips and tricks to find out if they work in the game or not.

UNSPEAKABLEPLAYS
7.45 MILLION SUBS

8 Spinning off from his main channel, Unspeakable (aka Nathan Johnson Graham) has created a treasure trove of awesome Minecraft content. Find out how to play tricks on your friends, become a Minecraft pro and even try cooking Minecraft food in real life!

SSUNDEE
11.2 MILLION SUBS

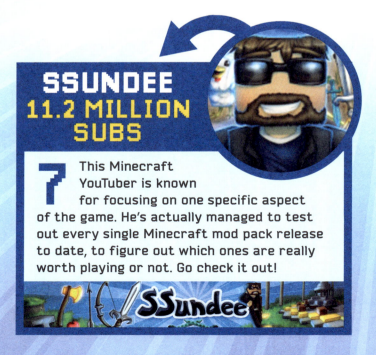

7 This Minecraft YouTuber is known for focusing on one specific aspect of the game. He's actually managed to test out every single Minecraft mod pack release to date, to figure out which ones are really worth playing or not. Go check it out!

CAPTAINSPARKLEZ
11.4 MILLION SUBS

6 One of the best Minecraft YouTubers out there, CaptainSparklez is actually Jordan Maron, a gamer who launched his channel in 2010. His content is incredibly popular and includes reaction videos and even covers of famous songs.

WIEDERDUDE
12.9 MILLION SUBS

5 This is another great YouTube channel, one that's known by fans for its tutorials and Noob vs. Pro videos. WiederDude also completes the same challenge over and over again at different skill levels, teaching gamers how to become better players.

PRESTONPLAYZ
14.4 MILLION SUBS

4 Heading into the top three is PrestonPlayz, whose millions of devoted fans regularly tune in to his channel to see what's new. Preston Blaine Arsement started creating YouTube content back in 2012 and is part of the Minecraft community known as 'The Pack.'

APHMAU
17.2 MILLION SUBS

3 Famous for her Minecraft role-play videos, Jessica Bravura's hilarious stories feature her characters and friends in various quirky worlds and situations. These imaginative tales combine romance, drama and comedy and are a huge hit with her fanbase.

JELLY
23.4 MILLION SUBS

2 Jelly's real name is Jelle Van Vucht, a Dutch YouTuber who started making videos when he was just 17 years old. His Minecraft content is very funny and he releases multiple new videos on his channel every single week.

DREAM
31.5 MILLION SUBS

1 When it comes to being the king of YouTube content, Dream is in a league of his own. With over 31.5 million subscribers, his videos include incredibly skilful play and world record-setting playthroughs that are a sight to behold. Go check him out!

MINECRAFT
FACTS & SECRETS

Amaze your friends with these awesome facts all about the biggest video game in the world, Mojang's Minecraft!

Once every 10,000 times you play, a 'Minceraft' typo appears on the title screen.

One day in Minecraft actually equals 20 minutes in real-time.

Minecraft was originally going to be called 'Cave Game'!

Minecraft has over 140 million active monthly players.

It's impossible to hit an Enderman with eggs or snowballs!

Minecraft creator Markus Persson created the first version of the game in just six days.

Ghasts are in fact voiced by Minecraft music producer Daniel Rosenfeld's cat!

In 2014, Microsoft bought Minecraft from Mojang for $2.5 billion.

There are currently 107 achievements to unlock in Minecraft.

Wear a pumpkin on your head and you'll become invisible to Endermen!

The largest city ever built in Minecraft was constructed from over 500 million blocks.

Minecraft has generated over $3 billion since it launched in 2011.

Over 20% of Minecraft players are based in the USA, followed by Brazil with 6.17%.

More than 300 million copies of Minecraft have been sold so far!